The War of the Spanish Succession: The History of the Co[nflict between the] Bourbons and Habsburgs that Engulfed Eur[ope]

By Charles River Editors

François Gérard's painting of Philip of Anjou being proclaimed King Philip V of Spain

About Charles River Editors

Charles River Editors is a boutique digital publishing company, specializing in bringing history back to life with educational and engaging books on a wide range of topics. Keep up to date with our new and free offerings with this 5 second sign up on our weekly mailing list, and visit Our Kindle Author Page to see other recently published Kindle titles.

We make these books for you and always want to know our readers' opinions, so we encourage you to leave reviews and look forward to publishing new and exciting titles each week.

Introduction

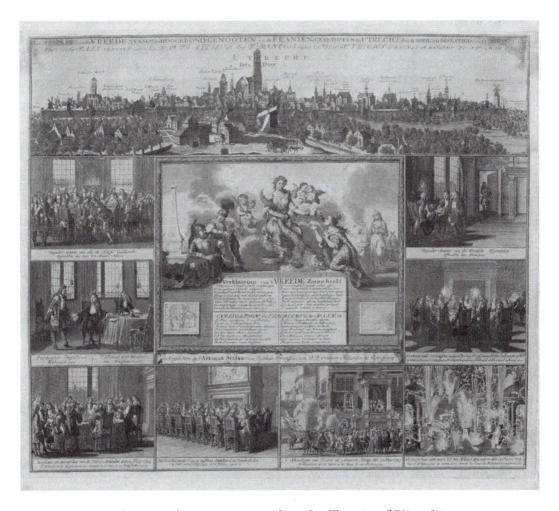

A portrait commemorating the Treaty of Utrecht

The War of the Spanish Succession, fought at the beginning of the 18th century, was the last major war engaged in by French King Louis XIV, the legendary Sun King, and it was also the most famous of all military conflicts during his reign. While the length and the scope of the conflict are the primary reasons why people have given so much attention to it, another reason for its historical popularity is no doubt the fact that its outcome humbled the French king, to the delight of his many critics. He was, after all, the one who had given himself the lofty nickname of "the Sun King."

During this lengthy European conflict, King Louis XIV of the Bourbon dynasty was pitted against Emperor Leopold of the Habsburg Dynasty of Austria, as well as Leopold's British and Dutch Allies. Lasting 13 years, the war spread from France and Austria to involve countries across the globe, and all of it centered on what would become of Spain's massive empire after the death of King Carlos II, who had no obvious successor to his crown. As an only child who had no children himself, Carlos II had been sickly his entire life, but as enfeebled as he was, he did preside over a rich empire that spread all the way across the Iberian Peninsula and included European territories in Italy and the Low Countries, land in North Africa, North and South America, and even as far away as the Philippines. Such an immense and wealthy empire needed a ruler, and as King Carlos II aged and weakened, everyone wanted to know who that would be.

Considering the age-old rivalry between the kingdom of France and the Austrian Empire, it is no surprise that those two powers both set their sights on the Spanish throne. As each side started to advance a claim that they were the legitimate heir to the throne, the initial idea across the continent was to find a peaceable solution that would manage to avoid a full-blown conflict. At the end of the 17th century, it seemed as though diplomacy would prevail, and that King Louis XIV would emerge victorious, but the prideful king made some unexpected mistakes that pushed the continent and then the globe into a lengthy war.

Indeed, the War of the Spanish Succession ended up being one of the largest wars the world had ever seen, with fighting taking place all across Western Europe, southern Germany, the Balearic Islands in the Mediterranean, a significant portion of the Italian Peninsula, and even Scotland, the West Indies, and French Canada. Despite the massive scope of the conflict and the magnitude of the stakes, historians mostly concur that the War of the Spanish Succession was fought in a civilized manner, such that even prisoners of war were well treated, generally speaking. The generals in command on each side actually knew one another, counting some of their "enemies" as friends and even family.

When the war finally came to an end, the Spanish people found themselves happy with the king who declared victory, a satisfactory solution after 13 bloody and expensive years. *The War of the Spanish Succession: The History of the Conflict Between the Bourbons and Habsburgs that Engulfed Europe* looks at the events that brought about the war, the major battles, and the results. Along with pictures depicting important people, places, and events, you will learn about the War of the Spanish Succession like never before.

The War of the Spanish Succession: The History of the Conflict Between the Bourbons and Habsburgs that Engulfed Europe

About Charles River Editors

Introduction

    The Rise of the Sun King

    Jockeying for Position

    The Succession Crisis

    The Start of the War

    The French Attempt to Turn the Tide

    The Long Road to Peace

    Online Resources

    Bibliography

Free Books by Charles River Editors

Discounted Books by Charles River Editors

The Rise of the Sun King

France's most famous king, and Europe's longest serving monarch, King Louis XIV (1638-1715) is often viewed today as a symbol of royal extravagance and splendor. Reigning for over 72 years, the legacy of the "Sun King" is remembered for the magnificent Palace of Versailles, the patronizing of arts and theater, and the apocryphal quote "L'Etat c'est moi" ("I am the State").

Although it is more than fair to associate the Sun King with vanity and unfathomable spending on luxuries, the focus on the superficial aspects of the man and his reign have come to overshadow just how effective he was as a ruler. Becoming king as a child and assuming actual power in his early 20s, Louis spent nearly 55 years centralizing and consolidating power in his monarchy by bringing the aristocracy to heel and keeping religious divisions from devolving into violence, thereby passing off to his successor an absolute monarchy with a very solid foundation. At the same time, his foreign policies, though often criticized as quests for glory, helped establish France as the dominant power on the European continent and firmly in control of an overseas colonial empire that stretched both east and west. And of course, while his spending and extravagance are viewed critically today, his construction of = Europe's most famous palace and his patronizing of the arts established the kind of culture and society that France is still famous for across the world today.

King Louis XIV by Hyacinthe Rigaud (1701)

The Sun King's parents, Louis XIII and Anne of Austria, were married in their early teens. Like all royal marriages, theirs was a political one, joining the French Bourbon dynasty and the Spanish Habsburgs, and though the queen herself was called Anne of Austria, she never actually visited Austria during his reign. While the marriage was consummated immediately, the two then went several years without having relations. Louis XIII was often ill, suffering from significant intestinal issues, and typically preferred the company of his male favorites and later mistresses to that of his wife. Even when marital relations resumed, Anne did not conceive, suffering no less than four stillbirths from 1619-1631.

As he was still childless, Louis XIII's Bourbon line was practically in crisis mode as the couple reached their 30s, to the extent that the French people prayed for the royal couple and Anne herself was compelled to make pilgrimages and visit a number of shrines. Finally, when Anne was 36, she became pregnant, and on September 4, 1638, Anne delivered a healthy baby boy. Louis XIV was, like all royal children, born in full view of the court, and it was all the more special because he was the first male child born to the Bourbon dynasty in more than 30 years.

As an infant, Louis was often referred to as "God-given". Just two years later, Anne bore a second son, Phillipe.

Louis XIII

Queen Anne with Louis XIV and Philippe I, Duke of Orléans

By May 1643, Louis XIII was on his deathbed, and he had the 4-year-old Dauphin Louis brought to him. Upon asking the young child if he knew who he was, his son replied, "Louis the Fourteenth, Father." His father replied, "You are not Louis the Fourteenth yet." King Louis XIII died on May 14, 1643, likely from tuberculosis, and at four years and eight months, Louis XIV became the king.

Louis XIII had succeeded his assassinated father as a child and came of age with a regent council controlling power until he was in his late teens. Thus, in his will he tried to establish a similar model for his young son. Upon his death, however, Anne of Austria had his will annulled, which had the effect of doing away with a regent council, thereby making her the sole regent. Even still, the child king had a happier childhood than many royal children. Following his father's death, his close relationship with his mother continued, even as she effectively ruled. Anne took a strong interest in his education and upbringing, ensuring Louis was provided an academic education, a religious one, a social one, and a physical one. The young king was well-read, taught to be pious and devout, and socially cultured. He was also encouraged to ride, hunt, and swim.

While Anne's early regency was successful, including a significant victory against the Spanish, uprisings in Paris caused challenges later in her regency. The Fronde Parlementaire began in 1648, five years into Anne of Austria's regency for her young son. Under Louis XIII, the power of the Parlement de Paris had been limited, increasing the absolute power of the king, and in 1648, acting on the policies of his predecessor, Cardinal Mazarin arrested the leaders of Parlement. In response to that step, however, the people of Paris reacted violently, with insurrection and rioting, and the nobles wanted the king to call the Estates General. Faced with growing turmoil and no available army, the royal family and their followers fled Paris in October 1648. A peace treaty with Spain in 1648 allowed the French army to focus its attention on Paris. After a brief siege, the rebelling nobles and royal family signed the Peace of Rueil. This peace lasted until the end of 1649.

Cardinal Mazarin

The Peace of Rueil allowed the rebelling nobles, including the Prince of Conde and Prince of Conti, to come back to court, and naturally political intrigues began at once, particularly against Cardinal Mazarin. In January 1650, Mazarin arrested several key members of the nobility, including Conde and Conti, which induced a prominent French general, Turenne, to seek Spanish assistance and fight back to free Conde and Conti. Turenne's army, temporarily reinforced by Spain, took up arms in the south of France, but the Spanish forces withdrew before the battle and Turenne's army was defeated. A tenuous peace resulted, and the queen, as regent, pardoned the imprisoned princes and Turenne. Nevertheless, Cardinal Mazarin, realizing he held a very tenuous position, fled France, all but leaving no one at all in control. Anne of Austria lacked her trusted advisor, and the king was not yet old enough to rule.

Louis XIV reached his majority and became king in his own right in September 1651, an incredibly turbulent time for the French nobility. While he was in exile, Cardinal Mazarin raised a small army and returned to France in December 1651, opposed by Conde, who had maintained a close alliance with Spain upon being released from prison. The Franco-Spanish war continued on French ground throughout 1651, and after a battle in July 1652 for the city of Paris, the opposing nobility were backed against the gates. The nobles were spared by a noblewoman, the king's cousin, who ordered the gates of the city opened, offering the rebelling nobles the opportunity to escape. She herself manned the guns on the tower of the fortress of the Bastille.

This battle resulted in significant fractures within the nobility and royal family, as well king Mazarin's return to exile. The nobility established a government in the city, keeping the king outside the walls, but in October 1652, the bourgeois of the city opened the gates to the king. The rebellion eventually led to exile for many of those involved in opposing the rights of the king to rule, and Cardinal Mazarin reclaimed his official standing as chief minister to the young king. Like Richelieu, Mazarin was proving to have nine lives.

A 1655 portrait of Louis XIV as Jupiter, symbolizing that he was the Victor of the Fronde

While Louis had held the right to political power since his 13th birthday, his coronation took place on June 7, 1654. The grand affair lasted for hours at the Cathedral of Rheims, the traditional choice for the crowning of a French monarch, with Anne of Austria watching from a box at the sidelines. Though Anne retained a great deal of power within the court and over her son, that power began to gradually fade as the king grew older and bolder.

Louis first presented himself as a "Sun King" in a 1653 ballet, the Ballet of the Night. Known for his dancing skill, the young king was especially attractive, with long flowing hair he inherited from his mother, and he was considered quite charming. He regularly performed in court ballets, theatrical productions, and operas, choosing characters ranging from Apollo to a sorcerer. At only 14, Louis began flirtations and romances with various ladies of the court, including the nieces of Cardinal Mazarin, the Mancinis, who were renowned around France for their wit and beauty. Around this time, Louis likely carried on a sexual relationship with one of the queen's ladies.

Court romances aside, Louis XIV was, without a doubt, the most eligible possible bachelor for the daughters of European royalty. Given the conflict between Spain and France in the mid-17th century, the Spanish and French-born Maria Teresa was the expected candidate. Louis and Maria Theresa were born within days of one another, and there was an expectation, throughout their lives, that they would marry. Other possibilities, many cousins or distant cousins, included an English princess raised in France, Henriette-Anne.

While Anne of Austria and Cardinal Mazarin concerned themselves with his marriage, Louis focused on relationships with a variety of young women, including another of Mazarin's nieces, Marie Mancini. There is no evidence that the relationship was sexual, but the king did wish to marry Marie. She was eventually exiled and married to a Prince Colonna of Italy, who was surprised to find his wife was still a virgin.

Tensions continued between France and Spain, resulting in a short alliance with England, which at the time was currently ruled by Lord Protector Oliver Cromwell. As French and Spanish troops clashed, the king insisted upon remaining with his troops, but he became seriously ill in 1658 while at the front, likely with typhoid fever. While he recovered, his illness brought the need for a wife and heir to the forefront. After his recovery, Mazarin arranged for the king to meet with a princess of Savoy, Marguerite-Yolande, but just as marriage negotiations began, Philip IV of Spain offered his Infanta, Maria Teresa.

Maria Teresa as Infanta

Louis had been raised a good Catholic and welcomed marriage and children with good spirits, so in due course Maria Teresa became Queen Marie-Therese. The young woman was plump, with desirably fair skin and bright eyes. While pretty enough, she had not been taught French and could not dance, making her ill-prepared for her future with Louis XIV and the lively French court.

The marriage contract was substantial and complex, arranged in the hopes that Spain and France would be perpetually bound to each other, with the latter being the dominant force. Prior to the marriage ceremony, Maria Teresa renounced her rights to the Spanish succession, but a clause in the contract could restore those rights: if her dowry was not paid, she regained the right to inherit. A proxy marriage formalized the agreement until the official ceremony took place on June 9, 1660, as was traditional for a royal marriage. The new queen would not begin her journey to France until after the proxy marriage took place.

Depiction of the young queen being handed over by proxy to the French

The couple met for the first time when the young queen arrived, and they were married at once. The young couple consummated their marriage that night, with a royal bedding ceremony. Unlike many new royal couples who were young and had never met each other before, Louis XIV and his new queen were sexually compatible according to contemporary accounts, and Louis spent many nights in his bride's bed. She rose each morning and took communion as she prayed for a child after they had been together. Like all other aspects of royal life, their sex life was a public matter. When the royal couple entered Paris together for the first time in late August 1660, they were joyfully welcomed.

While Marie-Therese certainly met her wifely obligations, she was not a terribly intelligent or vivacious young woman and thus did not embrace her social role as French queen. Devoutly pious, she traveled with Anne of Austria to convents and religious sites, and Marie-Therese enjoyed gambling, which actually helped enhance her standing as queen. However, Marie-Therese spent much of her time surrounded by a small Spanish retinue, and she never learned to speak French, communicating with the well-educated and multilingual king solely in Spanish instead.

Marie-Therese became pregnant in early 1661, delivering a healthy son, and she was pregnant again within weeks, delivering a daughter who did not live. A second daughter lived only six weeks. The queen bore two more children in January 1667 and August 1668, but only the Dauphin survived early childhood.

Anne of Austria and Marie-Therese with the Dauphin

Cardinal Mazarin died on March 9, 1661, at which point Louis XIV made the astonishing announcement that he alone would preside over the government and there would be no replacement for Mazarin. Louis did retain a Royal Council, as well as several ministers, but none of them had the power to actually make decisions.

To be fair, Louis worked hard and devoted hours to ruling the kingdom. He paid close attention to detail, from military structure and order to the design of his palaces. Louis may never have actually claimed to be the state, but he was clearly determined to rule that way. To this end, Louis shrewdly drew his ministers from the ranks of the lower nobility, rather than the highest. From his first declaration upon the death of Cardinal Mazarin, Louis made clear his intention to keep his ministers and council subservient. They were to issue no commands and take no action without his orders and consent. The French king had chosen this course of action knowing full well that members of the higher nobility possessed too much wealth and power to dutifully remain servants to the King's will on his council.

Jockeying for Position

Along with the marriage, the Treaty of the Pyrenees, an agreement that brought peace to France and Spain, aimed to establish unity. In order to underscore their mutual importance, the marriage and the treaty were announced simultaneously, but almost from the minute the marriage was completed, King Louis XIV was already questioning the legitimacy of her renunciation. His critique of the agreement gained strength because Spain's King Philip IV failed to live up to his end of the bargain and pay the astronomical sum within the required time. Louis XIV felt justified in starting to threaten Spain because of the lack of payment, but from a technical perspective the 500,000 gold crowns were not meant as a direct quid pro quo: they were just a wedding "gift." The renunciation was only the implicit subtext, and in any case, the matter of the Spanish succession was far from settled. The unpaid sum only heightened the uncertainty surrounding the future of the Spanish Empire.

Philip IV

Philip IV and his wife, Maria Anna, had their own child, Carlos, who was the official, direct heir to the throne. Born in ill-health, Carlos had a very short life expectancy from the start, so despite his status as heir, Louis XIV continued to act as though the Spanish throne would soon be vacant, and his to claim. The French king's first act of aggression was to take Spanish territory in the Low Countries, and he tried to justify his military incursions based on the violation of his wife's "rights" and the lack of payment on the dowry.

The Franco-Dutch War began in 1672, and in this conflict, the French were allied with Sweden, Munster, Cologne, and England. Though the initial fighting involved only the Dutch

Republic, a later alliance between the Dutch Republic and Austria, Spain, and Brandenburg expanded the scope of the war. Louis XIV disliked many things about the Dutch Republic, some of them quite personally. While religious differences came into play, the Dutch government and lack of respect for monarchy was a central factor in this fight. The French secured strong initial victories, before alliance forces on the Dutch side pushed them back. Fighting continued for six years.

The Franco-Dutch war ended with the Treaty of Nijmegen in 1678, providing the French with additional lands formerly controlled by the Spanish, but the Franco-Dutch war is not considered a decisive French victory. The leader of the Dutch Republic, William of Orange, retained control, and it ensured the rivalry between Louis XIV and William continued. Still, the Franco-Dutch war did weaken the Spanish and successfully established France as the prominent military power of the 17th century.

In secret, Louis XIV had also reached an understanding with Austria's Emperor Leopold I. The two men were both grandsons of Philip III of Spain and thus felt equally entitled to inherit the Spanish Empire. Ultimately, they agreed they would divide it amongst themselves as soon as Carlos (who inherited the throne at four years of age) died. Carlos suffered from seemingly too many disabilities to count, likely the result of inbreeding, so the maneuvering certainly must have made sense to the other European rulers. As 20th century British author John Langdon-Davies famously put it, "We are dealing with a man who died of poison two hundred years before he was born. If birth is a beginning, of no man was it more true to say that in his beginning was his end. From the day of his birth they were waiting for his death."

Leopold I

This highly questionable diplomatic arrangement was made without any regard to what the Spanish people might have wanted for themselves, but most importantly, despite the poor prognostications about Carlos II's health, he continued to live on well past his predicted life expectancy.

Carlos II

The European balance of power shifted in 1689, when William of Orange took the throne of England as William II. The following year, he concluded an agreement with the Low Countries that Emperor Leopold should be given the Spanish throne after the death of Carlos II (assuming he never produced an heir).

William of Orange

    However, another series of events shifted the dynamic to a more neutral solution when the Nine Years' War broke out in Europe. In 1686, an anti-French alliance formed, made up of a number of other European powers including Spain, Austria, and Bavaria. Louis used the League of Augsburg as an excuse to take up arms, and in 1688, the French launched an attack on Germany. The War of the League of Augsburg would devastate Germany, destroy cities, and have a huge cost in both lives and money. In 1692, a significant portion of the French court, including Louis, joined the army at Namur on the Meuse River, only to find the conditions were quite poor. The royal servants had difficulty getting bread, the water quality was bad, and the wine was not good.

A painting depicting Louis at the Siege of Namur

The war finally ended with the Treaty of Ryswick in 1697. According to the terms, the neutral figure of Joseph Ferdinand, the young grandson of Carlos II's sister Margaret Theresa, would be put on the Spanish throne once it was vacated. This choice was considered a compromise that would keep the balance of power between Austria and France as stable as possible. As part of the treaty (which was considered to be equitable), Louis XIV's oldest son would get significant territories in southern Italy (including Sicily and Naples), and the Austrian emperor's son would get Luxembourg and the region of northern Italy that included Milan. In addition to this consolation prize, the countries negotiated trading deals that would give England and Holland a greater advantage in the Spanish Empire of the Indies.

Joseph Ferdinand

Beyond the territorial agreement, the major impact of the war on Louis XIV was that it instilled in him a hatred of war. After nine long years that worked to deplete his treasury, he left the conflict feeling as though war was a never-ending process. For this reason, he was happy to sign a treaty, even though it came up short in terms of how it would handle any of Carlos II's personal decisions about his inheritance if those decisions contradicted France and Austria's wishes. While Louis XIV was satisfied with the deal, Emperor Leopold I, on the contrary, thought that he had lost too much ground in signing it, considering the fact that before the war he had signed his own pact with William III that would have put him directly on the Spanish throne. Similarly dismayed were the Spanish aristocrats, who did not want their empire divided for any reason, especially not at the behest of foreign rulers who were divvying up Spanish territory as if it were birthday cake at a child's party.

Thus, in response to all this unrest amongst the nobility, Carlos II wrote a new will in 1698 that gave his throne to Joseph Ferdinand along with the entire Spanish Empire. Although his will was in complete defiance of the wishes of the other European powers, Carlos II was completely within his rights to make such a bequest, and so the plans were set. The other powers could do nothing to change the will by diplomatic negotiations, and no one was willing to jump back into another war.

As fate would have it, this solution only stayed in place for a short time because Joseph Ferdinand's life was cut abruptly short. Less than three months after Carlos II signed his new will, the child seemingly contracted smallpox on a visit to the Netherlands and died in February 1699. Some speculated he was poisoned, but regardless of the cause of death, Louis XIV and William III were quickly back in action, and they signed another agreement that would put Archduke Charles of Austria (the second son of the emperor) on the throne, on the condition that Spain could never be incorporated into the Austrian Empire. Once again, significant Italian territory was to go to the son of Louis XIV, this time including the coveted Milanese territory as well.

Archduke Charles

Emperor Leopold I should have been happy that his son was being offered the possibility of ruling Spain, but his anxiety over the expansion of French power in Italy caused him to reject the treaty that England, France and Holland all signed in March 1700. Fixated on the idea that Austria needed more territory in Italy, he stood his ground and refused to give in to the entreaties of England and Holland to join them in securing European peace. The other rulers thought he was being foolhardy, insofar as Austria stood to gain much more than it was giving up, particularly because Austria desperately needed to avoid another war with France.

In the time that Emperor Leopold I was refusing to sign, more actors were stirring behind the scenes, including Duke Victor Amadeus II of Savoy, a distant cousin of Louis XIV who also claimed his rights to the Spanish throne through his grandmother's relation to King Philip II of Spain. Louis XIV used this moment of confusion and uncertainty to try to advance his own cause, using his ambassador to Spain to effectively lobby to promote French interests in that country. His new plan was to advance his second grandson, Philippe, Duc d'Anjou, as the rightful successor to Carlos II. In this plan he was helped by the fortuitous fact that the pro-Austrian faction in the Spanish court was not very diplomatically nimble. Eventually, despite Louis XIV's pessimism, his grandson was accepted as the heir to Carlos II, and Philippe even had the support of the Vatican, which saw him as the best candidate to maintain the fragile peace.

Philippe

The Succession Crisis

In 1700, the end of Carlos II's life was nearing, and in those final months, the pro-French faction of the court was able to isolate him and make sure that he had no contact with his German-born queen, who may have tried to shift his opinion. A new will was drawn up, and the Philippe was named Carlos II's successor. According to the terms, he would preside over an undivided empire. The second in the line of succession would be Louis XIV's younger grandson, the Duc de Berry, and the next in line would be the Archduke Charles of Austria, the second son of the emperor. Fourth in line would be Duke Victor Amadeus II of Savoy, and there was a regency that was to be established in Spain to govern in the interim between the end of Carlos II's life and the arrival of the new sovereign in Madrid.

In the last weeks of his life, Carlos II surprised everyone when he seemed to regain vitality, exhibiting a liveliness that he had rarely possessed during his sickly existence. His improved health was so striking that there was even talk in the court of a final hope that he would be able to impregnate his wife and leave a direct heir. However, those hopes proved to be in vain, and despite the temporary physical resurgence, Carlos II died on All Saints Day (November 1) in 1700. The official autopsy reported that when he died, the Spanish monarch's body "did not contain a single drop of blood; his heart was the size of a peppercorn; his lungs corroded; his intestines rotten and gangrenous; he had a single testicle, black as coal, and his head was full of water."

Despite having been plagued by poor health and having ruled during a time of relative hardship, Carlos II was mourned by the Spanish people, who mostly considered him a fair and kind king who capably shepherded them through a time of economic strife.

News of the king's death was sent to France via secret message, and despite the fact that he was now poised to realize his long-time dream of possessing the Spanish Empire, Louis XIV received it with apprehension. He was well aware of European politics, and that the revelation of the plan of succession would be taken as a betrayal by the Austrians. Moreover, in response to the dramatic news, Louis XIV's own son was surprisingly adamant that the throne belonged to him. He cited his mother's rightful claim to it since she was, in fact, the half-sister of Carlos II. The Dauphin agreed that he would not take the throne himself and instead pass it on to his son, Philippe, but he absolutely refused to concede anything else. Everyone expected that Louis XIV would support this decision, and he ultimately did out of fear that if he did not, the Austrians would take the throne themselves. With that, on November 12, 1700, Louis XIV communicated his acceptance of Carlos II's will, even as he worried about the rest of the continent's reaction to the news.

At this point, everything seemed stable. Philippe had a strong claim to legitimacy because of his grandmother's close familial relationship to Carlos II. Perhaps most importantly, nobody in position to contest him seemed to have an appetite for a new war. Even the Austrian emperor held his tongue about his own son's rights to the throne.

As the year 1700 ended, a crisis appeared to have been averted, and Philippe began his journey to Madrid to be crowned as King Philip V. Everything had been taken care of to make sure that there were no possible legal impediments to his arrival, and the final confidential clause in the Treaty of Partition that would have allowed Emperor Leopold I to contest the will had expired, so Philip's coronation seemed legally valid when he crossed into Spanish territory. When he arrived in Madrid in February 1701, the scene was festive and the new king was calm and confident. Carlos II's widow, Maria Anna of Neuburg, was sent off into retirement in Toledo in order to prevent her from stirring up trouble, and the entire court was purged of its Austrian influence. French men were appointed to the most important positions in the king's new council.

The next order of business was to find the 18-year-old king a wife, a decision in which he would have no say at all. After studying the political landscape, Louis XIV chose Marie Louise, the 13-year-old daughter of Duke Victor Amadeus II of Savoy, in the (ultimately misguided) hopes that it would help cement the alliance between Savoy and France. The marriage got off to a rocky start, as the young bride expected to be able to bring her own attendants with her to Spain, but eventually the young couple found a suitable dynamic between them. Despite Marie Louise's strong character, she became a trusted figure for Philip, and she was a loyal source of support for him during the war that was about to come.

Newly crowned, Philip set about his business of running the Spanish Empire, and he decided early on to visit Naples and meet his Italian subjects. The Italian people were not particularly excited about his arrival, and they did not care whether a Bourbon or Habsburg was on the throne. Even worse, his decision to go to Italy so soon after his coronation was not appreciated in Spain either, as his court felt that he needed to take care of business at home. Nonetheless, Philip's initial time on the throne seemed peaceful enough, with only Vienna denying his legitimacy, and there was no sign that England and Holland were interested in any way in starting a war in order to advance the interests of Austria, particularly because they now had an assurance that their trading routes in the Spanish Empire would be safeguarded and even possibly improved. In reality, the hopes of improving the trade deals actually did not come to pass, as the Spanish continued to favor French companies in their dealings, but England and Holland were so resistant to the idea of another war that they accepted these financial slights in order to avoid possible disaster.

Not only were there political reasons to leave the king alone, but there were military ones as well. Louis XIV had numerous allies across Europe, and the Iberian Peninsula was geographically difficult to attack, whereas Holland and Austria, the two countries that would be most likely to start an attack, were more vulnerable.

Around this time, fighting broke out in Milan, which was a territory that was very dear to France since it served as a buffer between Spain and Austria. Although the French troops fought valiantly, they were decimated by the Austrian imperial forces led by Prince Eugene of Savoy, who managed to gain significant Spanish territory in northern Italy. This conflict, considered the preamble to the War of the Spanish Succession, cast an ominous shadow across Europe, and it cast into doubt whether the French would be able to hold the Spanish throne. The rest of Europe was on alert, as it was now possible that the French would lash out at Holland to try to shore up their authority over the continent.

The Start of the War

In the wake of the fighting in northern Italy, hostilities broke out in the Spanish Netherlands when the local governor general, Maximilian Emanuel Wittelsbach, colluded with Louis XIV and essentially betrayed the Austrian Empire. Wittelsbach made this treacherous agreement because of a clause that Louis XIV put in their secret treaty which stated that the French would do their utmost to put Wittelsbach on the Austrian throne if given the opportunity. Although Wittelsbach had a reputation as an excellent soldier, his diplomatic skills proved lacking, and he let his ambition lead him to make an outrageous agreement that paved the way to war.

Wittelsbach

The French framed this military incursion as a strategy to help protect the territory of the newly crowned King Philip V, although William III was aware of the fact that Louis XIV was actually doing this for himself, not for his grandson. The unprovoked aggression angered the Dutch people, and though the French were able to stake their claim with virtually no violence, they had shifted the balance of power in a dramatic way and stirred up anti-French sentiment among the Dutch that would cost them in the long run. The move also antagonized the English people, who were closely aligned with their Dutch neighbors. Historians ascribe this unusually tone-deaf decision on the part of Louis XIV, who was generally known for his wisdom, to his own ambitions and his desire to bolster his family.

The French incursion served to shore up the alliance between England and Holland, two maritime powers whose lucrative trade deals were now suffering because the Spanish Empire was favoring the French. These two allies naturally turned to Austria, which had been primed and ready to join a coalition against the French ever since the news of Philip V's succession was made public. On September 7, 1701, the three countries formed a Grand Alliance, and in the coming months Denmark and the German states also signed treaties with the Grand Alliance for a variety of interests, including monetary ones. Foremost in everyone's mind was the fear that France would continue to grow more powerful and dominate Europe.

Despite Louis XIV's aggression, the tide had not turned completely against Philip V since his legitimacy was generally accepted by the rest of Europe. The problem was not the ruler, specifically, but the issue of the division of the Spanish Empire. Then Louis XIV made matters worse once again, this time by interfering in English politics. When his longtime friend, King James II, was on his sickbed in exile in St. Germaine, Louis XIV visited him and pledged that he would support the king's son, James Edward Stuart, in his attempt to take back the throne in London. This was a breach of international diplomacy and the Treaty of Ryswick of 1697, and the gaffe furthered the wider belief that Louis XIV was completely without scruples when it came to negotiations. The diplomatic relationship between France and England was cut off, and this only added fuel to the fire, as the French representative in London had been doing a particularly admirable job in keeping the English calm in the face of the French conduct.

Louis XIV held strong in the face of these turning tides because he thought he foresaw a number of favorable circumstances coming into focus. He figured that when William III (who was ailing at the time) died, he would be able to forge a better relationship with Holland. He also was confident that Emperor Leopold I was too busy trying to make territorial gains in northern Italy, fending off a rebellion in Hungary, and dealing with the perpetual threat of the Ottoman Turks to be interested in French matters.

To be fair, this was not a complete flight of fancy on Louis XIV's part. Indeed, the Dutch were worried about the fact that their Austrian allies were busy in Italy and would be unable to rush to their defense if France attacked Holland quickly, which the French monarch appeared to be getting ready to do. In November 1701, he sent troops north to occupy the Bishopric of Liege, followed by an occupation of Bon in the Bishopric of Cologne. These occupations successfully isolated the important Dutch territory of Maastricht.

The situation worsened when William III, one of Louis XIV's most forthright opponents, ended up dying in a tragic accident in March 1702 after falling off his horse and breaking his collarbone. The new queen, Princess Anne, who was William III's sister-in-law and the daughter of King James II, was celebrated upon her coronation in London. Again, Louis XIV assumed this would bring a change to the political scene, but that would not be the case - Queen Anne was intent on limiting French power and ensuring that the English crown remained in Protestant hands, two issues that were related since Louis had given his support to the Jacobite (Catholic) cause.

Less than two months after the death of William III, on May 15, 1702, a state of war with France, as well as with the French prince in Spain, was announced at the same time in London, The Hague, and Vienna. Queen Anne based her declaration on the Treaty of Grand Alliance, and the Dutch evoked the 1697 Treaty of Ryswick, which specified that the French would make no occupation of Dutch-held lands, a provision they violated when they seized those territories several months earlier. Emperor Leopold I of Austria also joined in with the rest of the alliance in declaring war, but it was a mere formality because his troops were already fighting against the French in northern Italy for some time. He evoked the Treaty of Ryswick in order to formally throw in his lot with his fellow members of the Grand Alliance. Their main objective was to secure peace in Europe by partitioning the Spanish Empire, a seemingly reasonable objective that they ended up deviating from during the course of the war.

Queen Anne

According to an anecdote, when Louis XIV received the formal declaration of war, he grew so angry that he threw the piece of parchment on the table and joked that he must be getting to be an old man for a woman such as Queen Anne to have declared war against him. Unfortunately for him, it was not a single woman who was about to wage war against him, but a formidable group of armies. England, Holland, and Austria had the support of Hanover, Brandenburg, Denmark, the bishoprics of Munster and Wurzburg, as well as the Electors of the Palatinate, Trier, Mainz and Mecklenburg Schwerin. Although the majority of all the other German princes were not actually ready to declare war on Louis XIV at the outset, they had no compunctions against sending their well-trained soldiers to fight alongside the alliance in return for payment.

In terms of allies, the deck appeared to be heavily stacked against Louis XIV, but the French actually had the military advantage in the early phase of the war. The French army was rather large in size and very well trained and equipped, and Louis had allies in Bavaria and Savoy who would be happy to have French troops on their land to threaten Vienna and the other German princes. France also had an alliance with Portugal, which helped them protect the Atlantic coast of the Iberian Peninsula. Moreover, the French had invested in heavily defending the northeast of their territory which, coupled with the natural defenses of the mountain ranges in the east and southeast of the country, made France hard to attack. Finally, the relationship with Spain would help to protect France's southern border, as long as Louis XIV sent his grandson a fair number of troops within a relatively short period of time. Thus, while the Grand Alliance did not have many military options, Louis XIV had plenty of possibilities in terms of where to make his first move.

At first, fighting was only taking place in northern Italy, with François de Neufville, the 2nd Duke of Villeroy, facing off against Prince Eugene of Savoy, who had been leading a successful campaign. However, Pope Clement XI threw his support in with the Bourbons, which meant that Prince Eugene started to have difficulties getting the supplies he needed for his troops. In order to respond to this increasingly dire situation, Prince Eugene intensified the aggression and seized the fortified city of Cremona, located on the Po River in the heart of French territory. This audacious strategy appeared to be successful when it resulted in the capture of a surprised (and half-naked) Villeroy. However, it was only a temporary victory, as the French counterattacked and Prince Eugene had to retreat. After his middling performance, Marshal Villeroy was replaced by a much savvier commander, Louis Joseph de Bourbon, Duke of Vendome, who gave Prince Eugene a much tougher fight than his predecessor.

Prince Eugene of Savoy

The 2nd Duke of Villeroy

The situation in Italy was not going well, but that was the least of the worries for the Grand Alliance. In plotting their initial strategy, the Grand Alliance feared that Louis XIV would think that Holland was the most convenient place for the first major French attack since the Spanish Netherlands had fallen to French troops. Worse, Queen Anne was relatively new on the throne, and whereas William III had been a staunch defender of Holland, the Dutch people feared that the new queen would not be good on her word. If southern Holland were to fall quickly, the war would surely be won by the French in short order.

Furthermore, the Grand Alliance also had serious issues to deal with at sea, and they made people question the wisdom of going to war with a power such as the French. Since Italy and

Spain had so many ports on the Mediterranean that were open to Louis XIV's ships, the British and the Dutch were at a major disadvantage on that crucial body of water. Beyond Europe, the French and Spanish traders had complete access to the Indies, while their enemies were slapped with a crippling trade embargo. The Grand Alliance was not even secure in the Caribbean, where the British had their outposts, including Jamaica, Barbados and the Bahamas, as these islands were vulnerable and open to attack. Admiral John Benbow, who had served previously in the Indies under William III, was sent to Jamaica in order to keep a careful watch on any possible French incursions. He faced his first challenge in the summer of 1702 when the French left a small squadron on the Colombian port town of Cartagena. They eventually engaged in battle, but several of his captains proved too cowardly to engage. Admiral Benbow ended up dying from wounds sustained in a battle that September, and his craven captains were executed by firing squad.

In order to gain a significant foothold in the Mediterranean, the British and the Dutch decided they needed to confront the threat posed by the city of Cadiz in southwestern Spain, where the Spanish navy had its base. The strategic location served as a port from which the French and Spanish could sail in order to block the Strait of Gibraltar, the key passage from the Mediterranean to the Atlantic through which valuable goods were regularly transported between the New World and Europe. If they were able to gain control of the port, the Grand Alliance would benefit immensely. First, they would deal a blow to Spanish trade and, thus, their economy. Second, they would be able to use that success to put pressure on Portugal as well as on Savoy, which would allow them regular access in and out of the Mediterranean. In fact, there was even hope of convincing Portugal to change sides at a certain point in the conflict. Third, they had the increased possibility of being able to inflict damage on the French since, in order to lend support to Cadiz, their naval fleet would have to travel the long distance from Toulon to reach the southwestern Mediterranean city. This not only meant Cadiz would not have French support for some time, but also that the French fleets would have to make themselves vulnerable in order to get there. Finally, once Cadiz was secured, the Grand Alliance calculated they would be able to work on gaining possession of Naples and weaken what seemed to be a growing alliance between the Vatican and Philip V, who had made a point to visit Naples early on in his reign - despite the complaints of his new bride and his new subjects - precisely for this diplomatic reason.

With so many clear reasons for attacking Cadiz, 50 warships from Britain and Holland sailed through the English Channel and down the coast of Portugal under the command of the British Admiral Sir George Rooke and the Dutch Lieutenant-Admiral van Allemond. They found no French squadrons on their journey, and they were feeling confident about their chances, especially since Sir Rooke had experience in Cadiz and thought that the town and the port were not particularly well defended. They landed in August 1702 after a chaotic discussion of how and where to land, coming ashore on a bay to the north of Cadiz on August 26 and facing no serious opposition from the locals in the nearby town of Rota. Some of the British and Dutch men did drown, however, due to choppy seas. Standing in Rota, the Grand Alliance read a proclamation that declared Archduke Charles the rightful king of Spain. A flag was raised, but the locals did not seem to provide much of a reaction to the provocative gesture.

Sir Rooke

For two days, the forces worked to unload all their men, guns, horses, and equipment, and then they took another week to prepare themselves to march to Cadiz. During this time of preparation, the British and Dutch soldiers started out by behaving rather civilly, with only one man executed for looting. However, when a group of soldiers happened upon a stash of wine, their commanders lost control of them, and the typical acts of looting and pillaging became commonplace. This was a major setback for the Grand Alliance, as the opinion of locals in the region went from being indifferent to being openly hostile to these invaders. In fact, the looting ended up having a major impact on Sir Rooke's ability to lead his advance on Cadiz because the summer weather was so hot and his troops had lost the goodwill of the people who could give them drinking water. Ultimately, the attack on Cadiz had to be called off, and by September 26 the decision had been made final. Although some wanted to bomb Cadiz as a final act of vengeance, cooler heads prevailed, and on September 28, most of the British and Dutch troops were on their way.

While they lost their bid for Cadiz, however, Sir Rooke found a new opportunity to seize a fleet of Spanish treasure a month later. The attack yielded six transports full of treasures and other goods, as well as the destruction of three other Spanish ships and 11 other transports. The attack also allowed the British to destroy the French squadron that had come to their allies' defense, which resulted in their loss of 16 warships. Thus, while the debacle in Cadiz dealt the Grand Alliance a major setback in terms of their efforts to control the Mediterranean, this unexpected success proved decisive in their bid to weaken France and deal a devastating financial blow to their fleet. Sir Rooke ended up with the equivalent of one million sterling, as well as prize money for their capture.

A depiction of the attack on the Spanish treasure fleet

At this point, the Grand Alliance had still not been able to convince the Portuguese to abandon the Spanish and join the Grand Alliance. With that in mind, a diplomatic campaign to pressure Portugal's King Pedro II was established. The fact that the Spanish and French navies were continuing to face difficulties in their battles was a powerful argument in favor of Portugal changing sides, as their sustained losses would open Portugal up to potential attack. Some of King Pedro II's advisers urged him to remain neutral, but he was concerned both about Portugal's territory and its overseas trade routes. He understood that the British and the Dutch could prove a serious threat to that lucrative source of income - and staying neutral would not be enough to incentivize them to leave those trade routes alone. King Pedro decided to negotiate between the Grand Alliance and Louis XIV in order to see who could offer him the best deal.

Pedro II of Portugal

When Portugal agreed to join the alliance, King Pedro managed to extract a number of concessions. First, Archduke Charles would go to Lisbon, along with an army of 12,000 troops. The Portuguese also demanded that, in order to protect against a possible Navy assault, an Anglo-Dutch cruising squadron be stationed on the Atlantic coast of Portugal. Furthermore, they demanded that the salaries of the Portuguese soldiers be paid for by the Grand Alliance, which was also required to outfit them. The Grand Alliance valued the addition of Portugal because of the strategic position it offered to allow access to the Mediterranean vis-a-vis the River Tagus (the longest in the Mediterranean). Ultimately, the terms were agreed upon, and King Pedro II officially chose to side with the Grand Alliance. They signed a treaty in May 1703, and it was ratified in July of that year.

While the fighting was going on at sea, in the spring of 1702 the French commander, Louis Francois de Boufflers, was attempting to defeat the Dutch army. His goal was to conquer the Low Countries before the troops of Queen Anne were able to get themselves prepared for battle. The idea was a good one because it would have opened up the southern border of Holland, key to Louis XIV's and Philip V's victory, and the plan was playing out rather well until June of that year, when John Churchill, the 1st Duke of Marlborough, was sent to lead the Anglo-Dutch forces. He proposed a more aggressive strategy, which concerned the Dutch generals, but he successfully got the rest of his allies on board over the course of the summer. By mid-August, the French were on the defensive, and in the fall, they started losing strategically important territories such as Liege. Marlborough managed to take many prisoners of war as well.

Marlborough

Marlborough proved his prowess on the battlefield that summer, but as he withdrew his troops for the winter, there was a lack of feeling of completion, as the tides had not been definitively turned yet. Moreover, the longer the war went, the more time Philip V was in position as Spain's king, and while he was not yet speaking Spanish proficiently or improving the bureaucracy of the Spanish court, he was well liked by the aristocrats and by the Spanish people.

Fighting reprised in the spring of 1703 as Marlborough decided to attack the French garrison in Bonn, which collapsed after 12 days of fighting. He then suffered a setback as he tried to join up with the Dutch troops, as they were unable to overtake the rapidly marching French. After suffering 4,000 casualties, he had to abandon his goal of taking Antwerp.

Marlborough then changed course and decided to attack French forces, specifically the town of Huy, which would allow him to reach the fortress of Namur. This fortress, since it was on a river, would provide its own strategic benefit in terms of allowing the allies to get access to supplies.

Winter weather came early that year, but by the end of September, Marlborough had achieved a number of important accomplishments. In his bombardment of Huy, he was able to explode one of the French warehouses and took 900 French troops prisoner. He eventually exchanged them for two allied battalions that had been lost earlier on in the campaign.

Failing to engage the French in direct battle, he chose to attack the minor fortress of Limburger, and then to finally capture the town of Guelders that he had been attempting to take since the spring. The end of fighting that fall saw the duke in an enviable position as his efforts in attacking the French and Spanish garrisons on the lower Rhine river meant that Holland was now protected enough to allow the Dutch commanders to have a chance to regroup and have their own successes. It also put the Spanish Netherlands at risk, and this territory was a prized possession of Philip V.

The only real success that the French managed to obtain that summer was on the upper Rhine river, a victory that earned them an important ally, the Elector of Bavaria, who would be able to help them isolate Vienna and expose it to an attack. Unfortunately for Louis XIV, however, this new relationship meant that he was obligated to send a fair number of troops in support when he actually had a greater need for them in the Low Countries or in northern Italy. The possibility of laying siege to Vienna and occupying it was tantalizing to Louis XIV and to Philip V, if only because the mere symbolism of it might be enough to stop the war. It would allow Louis XIV to consolidate his troops and attempt to retake the land in the southern Netherlands that he had so painfully lost. The Elector of Bavaria was also motivated to make this conquest of Vienna a reality, holding out his own hopes that Louis XIV would allow him to replace Emperor Leopold I.

They formulated a plan that would have the French and Bavarian troops advance through the Tyrol region with about 70,000 troops, but they encountered unexpected resistance from the Tyrolese people. They aimed to join another set of troops who were to pass through the Trentino region, but these troops too also failed in their efforts. The failure had its own unintended consequences, as the ambitious and savvy Duke Victor Amadeus II of Savoy, who had already been questioning his alliance with Louis XIV, took the moment to break off their relationship, violating not only a treaty obligation but also betraying his familial ties to the House of Bourbon. At this stage, even the French side's hold on the Rhine region was starting to weaken, and the alliance with the Elector of Bavaria in southern Germany seemed shaken as well.

Luckily for the French, the Grand Alliance was having its own troubles at the same time. A series of defeats in the fall of 1703 dimmed their prospects for a decisive, quick victory, and that winter, Louis XIV shored up eight different field armies, so it seemed the French were heading into 1704 with the upper hand despite their serious losses. Not only was Philip V growing ever stronger in Spain, the Dutch were starting to lose their appetite for war - they were happy enough to have secured their borders and did not want further conflict with France. On top of it, the British government was feeling the financial burdens and was demoralized by the French occupation of northern Italy, as well as the fortresses on the upper Rhine and the ongoing threat to Vienna. The only real place where the allies now had the advantage was on the sea, but no one believed that the sea would be decisive.

One of the most famous episodes of the War of the Spanish Succession took place in 1704 when the Duke of Marlborough led his army in a march up the Rhine. Although the Dutch were not keen to let the British commander leave the Low Countries so he could contribute to the war effort elsewhere, Marlborough felt he had no choice but to help protect Vienna and lend support to the imperial armies on the Danube. With the support of Bohemian diplomat Count Wratislaw, Marlborough conceived of a strategy, and in March of that year, he received the approval of Queen Anne, who was eager to show her support for her Austrian allies against the French and Bavarian threat.

At the same time, there was real concern about what would happen in southern Holland without Marlborough and his men, so it became a question of weighing the costs and benefits of him staying or going. Marlborough was persuasive in convincing the Dutch that his move would elicit a response from the French, and that they would feel compelled to follow him rather than stay behind and attack the weakened Dutch.

Preparations for the march were carried out in secret, and the men were poised to march quickly once they got underway. When Marshal Villeroy, who was commanding the French troops in the Low Countries, finally found out about Marlborough's movements, he was confused and sent word to Louis XIV, asking him how to respond. He did not understand why Marlborough would have left the border of southern Holland unprotected. As Marlborough had expected, Louis XIV responded quickly by telling Villeroy to go ahead and follow the enemy with his 20,000 troops.

As part of his plan, Marlborough made it seem as though he was heading for the Moselle Valley, but as soon as he caught wind of the fact that the French had responded as expected, he immediately changed his course, let go of the ruse that he was headed for the Moselle Valley, and instead crossed the east bank of the Rhine in May of that year. His next crossing, at the River Main, came less than a week later, and at this point it became clear that he was headed for Bavaria. Several days later, Marlborough and his men crossed the River Neckar, and only then did he admit to his own States General that he had always been meaning to go to the Danube. Although the Dutch had not been fully apprised of this intention when they originally accepted Marlborough's departure, they accepted the reality of the situation and even contributed troops to support the campaign, giving Marlborough 40,000 men to pit against whatever French formation he might face.

As Louis XIV responded to his generals' confusion, Marlborough was already meeting with the President of the Imperial War Council, Prince Eugene of Savoy, so they could plan for a joint campaign. Eugene would try to block the French from sending reinforcements to Bavaria, and Marlborough was to join forces with the Margrave of Baden in order to cut off the French and Bavarian armies, putting themselves between the enemy and the city of Vienna. Their union gave Marlborough 60,000 troops to command, but he still needed a good base that he could use to push his troops through the Danube. He settled on the town of Donauworth, which was located where the Danube and the River Wornitz joined together. It had everything the allies could want in a base, as it was easy to defend from the south, possessed a solid bridge over the Danube, and possessed a large set of storehouses where the allies could put all their supplies. The only downside was a rather large one: the French were not ignorant about these substantial advantages and had therefore established their own garrison in the town led by French Colonel DuBordet. Nearby, there were 12,000 French and Bavarian troops, and they were backed up by serious artillery forces led by a talented Piedmontese officer named Comte Jean d'Arco.

Marlborough and Baden knew they had to do something to gain possession of the garrison, which was located on the nearby Schellenberg hill, but they understood d'Arco's military prowess and feared they would suffer substantial casualties if they went for the garrison. The Margrave of Baden in particular was rather conservative in his strategy and had to be convinced by Marlborough to plow ahead. They attacked Schellenberg on July 2, costing them 5,000 troops between the dead and the seriously wounded. The Margrave of Baden was among the wounded after being shot in the foot, but the attack gave Marlborough the base he needed to cross over the Danube. The high level of casualties also earned him a great deal of criticism, but d'Arco's men suffered an even heavier defeat, with only 3,000 of his men escaping. Thus, in the overall balance of the war, the attack proved worthwhile, and Emperor Leopold I clearly concurred in his congratulatory message. Louis XIV was also of the opinion that Marlborough's attack had done much to set back the French cause.

With this victory under their belt, Marlborough and the wounded Baden crossed the Danube and into Bavaria, laying siege to the fortresses they passed on the way. When they could not persuade the Elector of Bavaria to break with Louis XIV, Marlborough set off a storm of fiery destruction across the countryside while prudently sparing the personal land of the Elector. Here, once again, the Margrave of Baden counseled a more restrained approach to Marlborough, but the duke had his way once again. He did not, however, cause the Elector to waver in his loyalty to the French. Thus, the duke's victory was incomplete, and the expectation was that he would have to return to the Low Countries in short order, which would leave Vienna vulnerable once again.

Marlborough's next remarkable move came in the summer of 1704 when he managed to unite with Prince Eugene of Savoy, who had been stationed with a force of 18,000 troops on the north bank of the Danube about 25 miles away from where Marlborough and Baden were with their larger army. Despite significant obstacles, they were able to mount a surprise attack on the French and the Bavarians, and though they suffered 12,000 casualties, they managed to destroy the enemy cavalry, capture 13,000 prisoners, and inflict about 20,000 casualties. One of their most prized captures was the French commander Marshal Camille d'Hostun de la Baume, the Duke of Tallard, along with a number of his senior officers. This devastating loss put Louis XIV's strategy under strain.

As England and Holland celebrated this unexpected victory, the French experienced their own shock over the defeat, which interrupted celebrations that had been ongoing for the recent birth of a son to the Dauphin, the Duc de Bourgogne and his wife. No one in the French court quite understood how Marlborough and his allies had managed to achieve their stunning success.

Marlborough's forces were greatly diminished, but he ended his victory by taking a tour through Berlin, Hanover, and The Hague, where he strategized with his allies and celebrated his success. He returned to London with a hero's welcome, and Parliament backed up lofty words of adulation with the authorization of the funds necessary to build him a palace.

The French Attempt to Turn the Tide

After this stunning success in the summer of 1704, one might have expected that 1705 would have been a banner year for the Grand Alliance, especially given the fact that Louis XIV would have to spend time rebuilding his severely depleted forces. However, when Emperor Leopold I died in May of that year, Vienna was faced with an unsettling transition despite the fact that the line of succession was clear. The late emperor's oldest son, Joseph I, would take the throne. Prince Eugene of Savoy also had to take time off from the war during that time to handle local diplomatic issues of his own. However, Prince Eugene and the new emperor benefited from a longstanding good rapport that would serve them well in the future.

Joseph I

After their defeats, Louis XIV rebuilt the French military, resorting to illegal drafts, increased taxes, and the purchase of a huge number of horses from Switzerland. This led to the French being able to field three armies in the Spanish Netherlands (commanded by Marshal Villeroy), the Moselle Valley (commanded by Marshal Villars), and Alsace (commanded by Marshal Marsin), an area where the Duke of Marlborough had made significant advances.

These reconstituted forces put Marlborough back on the defensive, and the Grand Alliance was not faring much better in Savoy and northern Italy. Prince Eugene of Savoy came in to personally supervise the headquarters in Turin, which helped raise the soldiers' flagging morale. Eugene devised to force the French into a war of diversion, such that they needed to keep 80,000 troops in Italy in order to continue to put pressure on the allies there while Eugene deployed only 40,000 men. Still, Prince Eugene's strategic calculations were not exact, and he ended up proving unable to keep his smaller army in the field. This forced him to withdraw into the neutral territory of Venice, where he faced the additional risk of angering the Venetians, who might choose to throw in their lot with the French. Eugene and Joseph were both convinced that Italy was the decisive theater, but it's unclear if this belief was motivated solely by their military analysis or by their personal desire to gain control of Italy.

With the hopes of bringing the Grand Alliance to the table for negotiations in the spring of 1706, the French decided to attack them on all fronts. This decision backfired, and Marlborough scored a major victory against Villeroy at Ramillies (in modern Belgium) in May, after which Louis XIV forced his old friend to resign and replaced him with the Duc de Vendome, who had been successfully campaigning in Italy. However, the pressure that the French had been mounting in Italy soon dissipated, and when the news of the French army's stunning loss at Ramillies spread through Europe, the Italian states breathed a sigh of relief, as they realized that Louis XIV's influence was waning.

The loss at Ramillies was essentially the deathblow to Louis XIV's offensive, and it forced the Sun King to go on the defensive in the hope that he could at least negotiate a favorable peace settlement. With virtually no chance of winning the war outright, his best hope strategically was to wage local campaigns to extract a better peace settlement and, in the meantime, hope that the allies made some kind of substantial mistake (though there was no sign that the experienced military commanders would do anything of the sort).

Louis XIV was reassured by the knowledge that he would be able to keep his grandson, Philip V, on the Spanish throne, and he was happy to agree that one of his other direct heirs would inherit his crown in France. He figured the allies would have no problem with that arrangement, and while they had been motivated by the fear that France and Spain would join their kingdoms, that unification seemed to be something the Spanish people themselves opposed.

As these machinations were being put in place, France's local offensives were unsuccessful. By September 1706, Louis XIV had suffered another humiliating and costly defeat, this time at the Siege of Turin, which compelled the French to withdraw from Italy completely. Vienna was now in control in Italy, free to disregard any of the Spanish or French claims on the peninsula. Having lost the southern Netherlands (which had been a great source of revenue) and northern Italy (which had been a highly strategic territory), Louis XIV and Philip V were in an unenviable position, with their treasuries depleted and the people's morale sinking.

A further loss at Oudenaarde (in modern Belgium) in July 1709 was the final straw for Louis XIV, who was fully willing to negotiate after losing 9,000 casualties and a further 9,000 prisoners at that battle. The loss of Oudenaarde allowed Marlborough to recapture Ghent and Bruges in January 1709, which forced the French to retreat to their own border during a bitterly cold winter that caused widespread famine across France and Spain, compounded by the interruption of their grain imports at the hands of the enemy navies.

The Long Road to Peace

Now that the Grand Alliance appeared to have won the war, the only task remaining was to try to secure peace. As it turned out, they did not excel at handling this delicate diplomatic task, which meant the war continued on while the diplomats and nobles bumbled around in their luxurious environments, making mistake after costly mistake as they tried to draft a document known as the Preliminaries of Hague. The allies' military success had gone to their heads, and they now felt confident to overshoot the terms of their original entry into the war. The British in particular were eager to kick King Philip V off the Spanish throne and install Archduke Charles on it, despite the fact the Grand Alliance had earned no military success in Spain itself. Worse, they included a clause that stipulated that Philip would receive no compensation for the throne, and that if he did not voluntarily step down within two months, the French themselves would be required to forcibly remove him. While the allies obviously hoped that Philip would just agree to abdicate, this absurd and humiliating request that Louis XIV be forced to go to war against his own grandson actually became public knowledge, spurring the kind of outrage that inspired the French king to decide to halt the negotiations and go back to war.

The casualties would continue to mount, and Marlborough earned several more victories, but even before peace negotiations could begin again in earnest, the war made its way beyond the borders of Europe and into the New World. In North America, Mohawk chiefs intervened on behalf of the British, assisting them in their hopes to gain territory in North America at the expense of the French.

With France greatly weakened but the Grand Alliance nonetheless unable to attack in any decisive manner, the negotiations started up, but it took an external event to finally end the constant back and forth and settle the question of Spanish succession. Emperor Joseph I died of smallpox on April 17, 1711 at the age of 34, compelling the allies to halt preparations for any future campaigns and deal with the question of his successor. The likely successor, Archduke Charles, was the very person the allies wanted to replace Philip V as Spain's king. He had to be formally elected, although he faced no realistic opposition, as the other candidate was the Elector of Bavaria, a staunch ally of Louis XIV and essentially a fugitive at that time. Thus, Archduke Charles became Holy Roman Emperor Charles VI, and he was crowned in Frankfurt in December of that year.

Now that Charles VI was the legitimate heir to all of the Austrian Habsburg territories, the balance of power shifted within the Grand Alliance, pushing it past the breaking point. Since Britain and Holland had been motivated to engage in war out of a desire to avoid allowing the French to consolidate too much power through their acquisition of the Spanish Empire, they certainly were not about to continue fighting a costly war to enable Charles VI to acquire the Spanish inheritance for himself. This would have effectively restored the Holy Roman Empire to its glory days under Charles V, who, in the early 1500s, ruled a collection of territories that included Germany, northern Italy, Austria, the Low Countries, all of Spain and its southern Italian territories, as well as Spanish and German colonies abroad. Moreover, because of the success of Prince Eugene and the Duke of Marlborough, the Spanish Empire was already effectively divided up, as large parts of the Low Countries and Italy were already being ruled by Austria. Suddenly, keeping Philip V on the throne would be the best way, in the view of the British and the Dutch, to maintain the balance of power in Europe.

The other major factor that weakened the Grand Alliance had to do with political maneuvers within the court of Queen Anne in London, where the enemies of the Duke of Marlborough gained the upper hand and, precisely at this crucial moment, managed to have him removed from power. The sidelining of this savvy, skilled leader caused much delight for Louis XIV, and it undoubtedly worked to his advantage when the time came for negotiations.

After several years of fighting, just about everyone agreed the war had dragged on too long. The need for securing a resolution further intensified as a series of deaths in the French court threatened to destabilize the line of succession. The Duc de Bourgogne (who had already lost his father to smallpox) died in a measles epidemic, as did his older son. Only his younger son, Louis, survived, and he would inherit the throne from his great-grandfather a few years later. Had he been killed by the measles as well, it would have set off another succession crisis by leaving Philip V of Spain as the only legitimate heir for the French monarchy, which would have united France and Spain.

Ultimately, the belligerents agreed to the Peace of Utrecht, a series of treaties signed between France and the other European powers, and between Spain and the other European powers. The fact that each of these countries had to enter into their own individual agreements was a sign of how fractured and contentious the European political scene remained after all those years of bloody conflict.

The Preliminary Articles that were drafted earned Great Britain a great deal. First, they awarded Britain substantial territory in North America from the French, including Newfoundland, Nova Scotia, the Hudson Bay territory, and the island of St. Kitts. The French also committed to destroying the fortifications they had built at Dunkirk, which had been strategically important to their efforts to sabotage the English and Dutch sea trade. Moreover, another part of the agreement would guarantee that the throne in London would remain in Protestant hands. France finally agreed to accept Queen Anne as the British sovereign and also agreed to stop supporting the restoration of James Edward, the son of the deposed King James II.

There were also concessions made to the Dutch to restore its southern barrier, and the French also signed a treaty with Prussia, in which France agreed to acknowledge the royal title of Frederick I and accept his territorial claims to Neufchâtel (today's Switzerland) and southeast Gelderland. Prussia, in return, gave France the principality of

Orange. France's concessions to Savoy included their recognition that Victor Amadeus II was to be Sicily's king, and they also granted him power over Nice. Even Portugal was able to extract concessions from the French, earning recognition of its sovereignty on both banks of the Amazon River.

The final major treaty that needed to be signed was between the new Holy Roman Emperor Charles VI and France. France and Austria continued to fight into the winter of 1713, but eventually Charles VI realized that the costs outweighed the benefits. The final treaty was a two-part endeavor, insofar as Charles VI first made peace in his own name (and Austria's) in Rastatt and then, six months later, entered into an agreement on behalf of the entire Holy Roman Empire at Baden in Switzerland. Crucial to this agreement was the fact that Charles VI renounce his claim to the Spanish throne (although he was entitled to keep his useless title of "King of Spain"), whereas the French also had to agree that the thrones of France and Spain would never be united.

While the French treaties began to be signed as early as April 1713, the Spanish treaties took a longer time to get in order. They granted Great Britain the status of "most favored nation" in their trading with Spain and its empire, and the agreements conceded that the territories of Gibraltar and Minorca would remain British. Moreover, Spain allowed Britain the exclusive right to handle the African slave trade with the Spanish colonies for a period of 30 years.

In their agreement with Savoy, the Spanish gave the kingdom of Sicily to Victor Amadeus in exchange for his formal renunciation of the Spanish throne. It was not until July 1714 that the Spanish signed a treaty with the Dutch, and they signed one with Portugal in February 1715.

Although the war was considered "over" with the signing of the Treaties of Rastatt and Baden between the Holy Roman Emperor Charles VI and France in 1714, the final agreements were not settled between the emperor and Spain until 1720 with the Treaty of The Hague.

Although Savoy, France, and Spain did manage to extract important concessions for themselves in the treaties and the Dutch and Portuguese got a few small advantages of their own, Great Britain was considered the biggest winner in the Peace of Utrecht. This would set the tone for the next several decades of European diplomacy. Due to its advantage on the seas, guaranteed thanks to its control of the ports of Gibraltar and Minorca, Britain was able to secure its status as the superior naval power, leaving the Dutch, Spanish, and Portuguese in their literal and metaphorical wake. Austria also emerged from the war greatly strengthened thanks to its newly secured territory in Italy, Hungary, and the majority of the Spanish Netherlands (although historians believe that Charles VI failed to fully capitalize on Austria's success because of his own myopic leadership).

France did manage to get a more beneficial settlement in the Peace of Utrecht than it would have had the negotiations of 1709 been successful. In a sense, that means Louis XIV was wise to continue on with the fighting for several more years. However, he may have had a moment of self-awareness on his deathbed. After leading his country into a conflict lasting 13 years, Louis XIV died in 1715, leaving the throne to his great grandson, Louis XV, who was only five at the time. The ailing king, according to the stories, finally conceded that he "loved war too well." Whether he actually uttered that, it is clear that he would have done well to avoid the Spanish War of Succession and stick with diplomacy. After all, the European geopolitics that the Sun King left Louis XV, who would rule until 1774, were not at all favorable to the French.

To be fair, the Sun King did leave his grandson Philip V in a relatively good position, and the war had managed to unite Spain and put a temporary hold on the separatist ambitions of people in Aragon, Valencia, and Catalonia. As a result, Philip V's position was Spain's leader was safe, even as Spain's global power was permanently waning. That had not been the case at all when the tentative young man arrived in Madrid less than 20 years earlier.

Sometimes referred to as the first world war of modern times, the War of the Spanish Succession was a harbinger of things to come as the various European powers competed for power across the globe. While the French had dominated Western Europe in the 17th century, the war brought an end to their dominance, and since the victors of the war typically write the history, the historical narrative was that the French and Spanish were deservedly brought to their knees.

Although the historiography of this lengthy war has been established for centuries, in the late 20th century, historians started to challenge this strongly anti-French narrative. They are now revisiting the notion that the French were actively trying to dominate all of Europe by pointing to recently uncovered evidence that underscores the extent to which they tried to avoid conflict. Moreover, Louis XIV cannot be faulted for his major decision to take the throne that had been vacated by the childless King Carlos II for his own grandson, rather than allow it to go to Archduke Charles, who would have used it to expand Austrian power. From this perspective, there are historians today who view the Spanish throne as a "poisoned chalice" that had the power to bring destruction to those who sought to obtain it. Although all the interested parties, including France, Spain, Austria, Holland, England, Portugal, Savoy, and Bavaria, claimed that they were averse to war, their conditions were too equivocal for that aversion to have any meaning. It may very well have been that the war was inevitable.

Perhaps even more remarkable than the drawn out nature of the War of the Spanish Succession is the fact that no one side could be properly declared the winner. After 13 years, all that was achieved was a shift in the balance of power. That said, despite the lack of a decisive resolution, this shift proved to be important for Europe, and the various powers were all compromised to an extent. That dynamic would make it possible for another legendary French leader, Napoleon Bonaparte, to rise out of the ashes of the French Revolution and shift the balance of power back to the French less than a century later.

Online Resources

Other books about Spanish history by Charles River Editors

Other books about French history by Charles River Editors

Other books about the War of the Spanish Succession on Amazon

Bibliography

Anderson, MS (1995). The War of Austrian Succession 1740–1748. Routledge. ISBN 978-0582059504.

Bromley, JS (1970). The New Cambridge Modern History: Volume 6, The Rise of Great Britain and Russia (1979 ed.). Cambridge University Press. ISBN 978-0521293969.

Carlos, Ann (author) Neal, Larry (author), Wandschneider, Kirsten (author) (2006). "The Origins of National Debt: The Financing and Re-financing of the War of the Spanish Succession". International Economic History Association.

Childs, John (1991). The Nine Years' War and the British Army, 1688–1697: The Operations in the Low Countries (2013 ed.). Manchester University Press. ISBN 0719089964.

Clodfelter, M. (2017). Warfare and Armed Conflicts: A Statistical Encyclopedia of Casualty and Other Figures, 1492–2015 (4th ed.). Jefferson, North Carolina: McFarland. ISBN 978-0786474707.

Colville, Alfred (1935). Studies in Anglo-French History During the Eighteenth, Nineteenth and Twentieth Centuries. Forgotten Books. ISBN 978-1528022392.

Cowans, Jon (2003). Modern Spain: A Documentary History. U. of Pennsylvania Press. ISBN 978-0-8122-1846-6.

Dadson, Trevor (ed), Thompson, Andrew (2014). The Utrecht Settlement and its Aftermath in Britain, Spain and the Treaty of Utrecht 1713–2013. Routledge. ISBN 978-1909662223.

de Vries, Jan (2009). "The Economic Crisis of the 17th Century". Journal of Interdisciplinary Studies. 40 (2).

Dhondt, Frederik, De Ruysscher, Capelle, K et al. (eds.) (2015). Historical Exempla in Legal Doctrine: the War of the Spanish Succession in Legal history, moving in new directions. Maklu. ISBN 9789046607589.

Elliott, John, Dadson, Trevor (ed) (2014). The Road to Utrecht in Britain, Spain and the Treaty of Utrecht 1713–2013. Routledge. ISBN 978-1909662223.

Falkner, James (2015). The War of the Spanish Succession 1701 – 1714. Pen & Sword. ISBN 978-1781590317.

Francis, David. The First Peninsular War 1702–1713. Ernest Benn Limited, 1975. ISBN 0510002056

Francis, David (May 1965). "Portugal and the Grand Alliance". Historical Research. 38 (97). doi:10.1111/j.1468-2281.1965.tb01638.x.

Frey, Linda; Frey, Marsha, eds. (1995). The Treaties of the War of the Spanish Succession: An Historical and Critical Dictionary. Greenwood. ISBN 978-0313278846.

Gregg, Edward (1980). Queen Anne (Revised) (The English Monarchs Series) (2001 ed.). Yale University Press. ISBN 978-0300090246.

Hochedlinger, Michael (2003). Austria's Wars of Emergence, 1683–1797. Routledge. ISBN 0582290848.

Holmes, Richard (2008). Marlborough: England's Fragile Genius. Harper. ISBN 978-0007225729.

Ingrao, Charles (1979). In Quest & Crisis; Emperor Joseph I and the Habsburg Monarchy (2010 ed.). Cambridge University Press. ISBN 978-0521785051.

Ingrao, Charles (2000). The Habsburg Monarchy, 1618–1815 (2010 ed.). Cambridge University Press. ISBN 978-0521785051.

Israel, Jonathan (1989). Dutch Primacy in World Trade, 1585–1740 (1990 ed.). Oxford University Press. ISBN 978-0198211396.

Kamen, Henry (2001). Philip V of Spain: The King Who Reigned Twice. Yale University Press. ISBN 978-0300180541.

Kann, Robert (1974). A History of the Habsburg Empire, 1526-1918 (1980 ed.). University of California Press. ISBN 978-0520042063.

Kubben, Raymond (2011). Regeneration and Hegemony; Franco-Batavian Relations in the Revolutionary Era 1795–1803. Martinus Nijhoff. ISBN 978-9004185586.

Lindsay, JO (1957). The New Cambridge Modern History: Volume 7, The Old Regime, 1713–1763. Cambridge University Press. ISBN 978-0521045452.

Lynn, John (1999). The Wars of Louis XIV, 1667–1714 (Modern Wars In Perspective). Longman. ISBN 978-0582056299.

McKay, Derek, Scott, HM (1983). The Rise of the Great Powers 1648 – 1815 (The Modern European State System). Routledge. ISBN 978-0582485549.

Meerts, Paul Willem (2014). Diplomatic negotiation: Essence and Evolution. http://hdl.handle.net/1887/29596: Leiden University dissertation.

Myers (1917). "Violation of Treaties: Bad Faith, Nonexecution and Disregard". The American Journal of International Law. 11 (4).

Ostwald, James, Murray & Sinnreich (ed) (2014). Creating the British way of war: English strategy in the War of the Spanish Succession in uccessful Strategies: Triumphing in War and Peace from Antiquity to the Present. Cambridge University Press. ISBN 978-1107633599.

Pincus, Steven. "Rethinking Mercantilism: Political Economy, The British Empire and the Atlantic World in the 17th and 18th Centuries". Warwick University.

Rule, John (2017). The Partition Treaties, 1698–1700 in A European View in Redefining William III: The Impact of the King-Stadholder in International Context. Routledge. ISBN 978-1138257962.

Schaeper, Thomas (March 1986). "French and English Trade after Utrecht". Journal for Eighteenth Century Studies. 9 (1). doi:10.1111/j.1754-0208.1986.tb00117.x.

Schmidt Voges, Inken (ed), Solana Crespo, Ana (ed) (2017). New Worlds?: Transformations in the Culture of International Relations Around the Peace of Utrecht in Politics and Culture in Europe, 1650–1750). Routledge. ISBN 978-1472463906.

Shinsuke, Satsuma (2013). Britain and Colonial Maritime War in the Early Eighteenth Century. Boydell Press. ISBN 978-1843838623.

Simms, Brendan (2008). Three Victories and a Defeat: The Rise and Fall of the First British Empire, 1714–1783. Penguin. ISBN 978-0140289848.

Somerset, Anne (2012). Queen Anne; the Politics of Passion. Harper. ISBN 978-0007203765.

Storrs, Christopher (2006). The Resilience of the Spanish Monarchy 1665–1700. OUP Oxford. ISBN 978-0199246373.

Sundstrom, Roy A (1992). Sidney Godolphin: Servant of the State. EDS Publications Ltd. ISBN 978-0874134384.

Symcox, Geoffrey (1985). Victor Amadeus; Absolutism in the Savoyard State, 1675–1730. University of California Press. ISBN 978-0520049741.

Szechi, Daniel (1994). The Jacobites: Britain and Europe, 1688–1788. Manchester University Press. ISBN 978-0719037740.

Thompson, RT (1973). Lothar Franz von Schönborn and the Diplomacy of the Electorate of Mainz:. Springer. ISBN 978-9024713462.

Vives, Jaime (1969). An Economic History of Spain. Princeton University Press. ISBN 978-0691051659.

Ward, William,, Leathes, Stanley (1912). The Cambridge Modern History (2010 ed.). Nabu. ISBN 978-1174382055.

White, Ian (2011). Rural Settlement 1500–1770 in The Oxford Companion to Scottish History. OUP. ISBN 978-0192116963.

Wolf, John (1968). Louis XIV (1974 ed.). WW Norton & Co. ISBN 978-0393007534.

Free Books by Charles River Editors

We have brand new titles available for free most days of the week. To see which of our titles are currently free, click on this link.

Discounted Books by Charles River Editors

We have titles at a discount price of just 99 cents everyday. To see which of our titles are currently 99 cents, click on this link.

Printed in Great Britain
by Amazon